APOCALYPSE CALYPSO

11/11/13.

APOCALYPSE CALYPSO

by

GRAHAM ROOS

Published in 2012 by
The University of Buckingham Press
Yeomanry House, Hunter Street
Buckingham MK18 1EG
United Kingdom

ISBN 9781908684042

To my Father
Kenneth Roos 1929 - 2011

GRAHAM ROOS

Graham Roos made his TV debut at the age of four and his theatre debut three years later at Theatre Royal, Lincoln. In 1981 he won the Art Scholarship to Rugby School. After studying at The Great Eastern Stage, he went to Buckingham University, reading English and History, where he wrote and directed his first play *A Study in Self Indulgence.* Settling in London in 1989 he has worked as voice over artist, lecturer and broadcaster.

His career has spanned the media of poetry, theatre, opera, music and film. His work has been performed both nationally and internationally and he has appeared on national and local television performing his work. Credits include the BBC; Channel 4; The Café de Paris; The British School, Rome; The ICA; Riverside Studios; Southwark Playhouse and King's Place.

Winner of the Magazine Design Awards in 2003 for his cult magazine *Large*, he has been nominated for The Somerset Maugham Prize and The Dennis Potter screenwriting Award.

His first book, *Rave*, was published by Oberon Books in 1998. *Quest*, his experimental CD of spoken word and music, was published in 2006 and features the voices of Fenella Fielding, Peter Wyngarde, James

Dreyfus, Martin Hancock and Sam Fox with music from Friends Lovers and Family.

Most recently he presented his black comedy *A son of Many Fathers* starring Derek Jacobi at the European School of Young Performers and his play *Her Holiness the Pope* was showcased at LAMDA in 2010. This year, as producer, director and writer, he has completed his first major film *Darkness:* a young rockstar is haunted by the poet Byron; starring Donald Sinden, Janet Suzman and Fenella Fielding.

ACKNOWLEDGEMENTS

I would first of all like to thank my long suffering mother for accepting the fact that I was never going to be a banker, doctor or lawyer despite the expensive education that was lavished on me. A big thank you is also due to Robin Dutt and Home House for giving me a regular platform from which to perform my work.

I would also like to thank the late Alan Sievewright FRSA for giving me the opportunity to develop a career in the arts, to Iain Deane for his steadfast friendship, guidance and support and also to Leon, Bertie and Elizabeth without whom my life would hold a lot less laughter.

Some of the poems in this book have already been published or recorded. *Twilight Speaks, Modern Dreams and Dilemmas, The Masks of Rome* and *Samson and the New World Order* are all tracks from my spoken word CD *Quest* (available on Itunes). *God is Not was* first published in *Sufi Magazine*. Other poems are new versions of poems previously published in my first book *Rave* (Oberon Books). The majority however are new works – many of which sprang from my work with the composer Dominic Muldowney at King's Place in 2009.

And finally, apologies to all three main UK

political parties as I have liberally and freely adapted the guff in their manifestos to give a convincing and authentic tone for the sort of rubbish spewed out in my very own Lucifer Party Manifesto which I use as theme headings in this book.

FOREWORD

Graham Roos' poetry is by turns lively, knowing, witty, wise and moving. Whilst never plummeting into mawkishness he has that gift of being able to ignite emotion, confront tragedy, celebrate loss with unseen tears and with a triumphant smile. It was the same when I first met him several years ago and gladly I can say, it remains so today.

I hold a seasonal Poetry Salon at Home House in London, a private members' club and have done so for the past dozen or so years. Graham was a most fitting and sparkling addition where he performed in the apple green and gilt eighteenth century Robert Adam splendour with such celebrated writers as the thankfully prolific Jeremy Reed and the late and controversially stupendous Sebastian Horsley. Several other talented writers and performers entertained the group and Roos became part of a fixture on these nights, holding the interest of his audience with grace and charm and always of course, with that trademark winning smile.

These three in particular lent their magic to those evenings and Roos, one might say, with his infectious enthusiasm, mischievous humour, delivery and on occasions, the screening of his 'film-poems', brought a sense of the purposefully dynamic and dramatic to the room.

Roos like the best poets transports the listener to that secret part of his or her understanding, so whilst the poet is very much in evidence, it is our magnetism to his words and the application of those dancing words to our lives that remains the strongest element. The page has a partner in the stage. Graham Roos performs on both and unites their identities.

ROBIN DUTT
Critic, Author (*Gilbert & George – Obsessions and Compulsions*) and Lecturer
HOME HOUSE
LONDON
February 2012

QUOTES

"Graham Roos has a way with words; his writing is vivid, catchy and thought-provoking. He leads the generation of young troubadours responding with verve to the world we have dumped on them."

Dame Janet Suzman: - Oscar nominee

"Graham Roos writes with a directness and urgency embracing both intellectual and emotional clarity. His characters are authentic and speak with individuality. He has an acute ear for pithy dialogue which is catchy, true, eminently 'sayable' with a fine mix of laughter and tears."

Sir Derek Jacobi: - British Actor

"Graham's showcase performance of 'Her Holiness the Pope' at LAMDA was completely absorbing from the opening moments. Even without benefit of scenery or costume the unfolding story of Pasqualina Lehrnhart's influence over Cardinal Eugenio Pacelli, later Pope Pius XII, was packed with dramatic tension and has a powerful resonance at the present time."

Dame Norma Major

"Graham Roos represents that rare being nowadays - someone with a very real talent and more importantly the elegant ability to demonstrate it whether on the silent page or through the inspired performance."

Robin Dutt: - Author, critic, broadcaster.

"Graham should have his own television show: he's Stephen Fry funny, James Dean photogenic and George Clooney charismatic. He has an irrepressible mischievous sense of humour and quite frankly has the most original mind of anyone I know."

Lucy Johnson: - Producer Channel 4 News

"No stone left unturned... pure originality... the depth of Graham's knowledge, experience, humour and humanity is inspiration itself. I thank him for finally making a brave step to publish his talents and collaborations on the net. Get this man to Broadway!"

Marina Crean: - New York Times Television.

"Graham Roos is very gifted. His range is wide - serious or satirical - on themes both topical and eternal. He wrote a piece in which I performed for Kings Place. The audience responded to the variety in it from start to finish, ending with prolonged applause. He has terrific energy and concentration."

Fenella Fielding: – British actress

"An original, inspirational writer, poet and performer, and a wizard when he wants to be, Graham Roos is a master of the unexpected, his work possessing a rare, visceral energy that tends to get into your veins. Buy him, devour him, beg your friends to do the same. Then bask in the glory of their gratitude. This man is destined for greatness."

Julie Alpine - Journalist and writer

PREFACE

This book began as an exploration of text and music with the composer Dominic Muldowney at The Royal Opera House and later at The London Sinfonietta. Under the aegis of *The Guardian,* this culminated in a series of events entitled *The Arts of News* at King's Place in 2009.

The aim of this event was to take stories from the newspapers and turn them into songs but without making the content "hieratic" and instead aiming to keep the journalistic, and often tabloid feel of the source.

From this commission two strands of work were produced. The first entitled *Songs of the Zeitgeist,* composed by Dominic and sung by Daniel Evans, was performed on the main stage at King's Place with the London Sinfonietta.

The other event that took place at The Box that week was my own work – *Songs of Reckoning*. This comprised work not included in *Zeitgeist* and formed a spoken word cabaret. Set in the Media Suite in Hell, Lucifer stands for election accompanied by the three Angles of the New Millennium. Lucifer was played by Benedict Hopper and the angels of the New Millennium were Janet Suzman, Fenella Fielding and myself. This show, directed by Di Trevis, incorporated previously unpublished material on similar themes of celebrity, excess, the passing of private life and a lust for thrills, including work from my CD of spoken word – *Quest*.

It is from these sources that this book originates. Some are clearly "demotic" and closer to popular song whilst others are "hieratic" using more traditional forms. But the themes of corruption and crisis blend together well, I hope, to make this a collection of poems for our time.

GRAHAM ROOS London 2012

CONTENTS

INTRODUCTION

Songs of the Zeitgeist was created in collaboration with the poet Graham Roos. The initial prompt was the fact that the London Sinfonietta was to relocate to a building that was also to house a daily national newspaper, *the Guardian*. This brought about the idea for a piece that attempted the unusual in contemporary music by tackling very recent topical news issues, basing its texts on newspaper articles.

I gave Graham Roos a list of all the things I was upset about or interested in – binge-drinking, trains, religion and war, Dawkins versus Creationism, CCTV, bees... It's a great opportunity to use sound effects, almost like trying to write for an exotic percussion instrument.

Song can put a dangerous spin on a subject. Composers so often reach for something like the Faber Book of Love Poems or Emily Dickinson and shun a topic because they are worried that it' s too topical, therefore too ephemeral, commonplace or quickly forgotten. Yet "art" can also be found under one's nose - on our doorstep, in a daily newspaper headline. It needn't be the result of a wearisome quest, the search for the "beautiful" that the 19th century insisted we make. In this project we've attempted to take hold of the "vernacular" and re-fashion it. The young understand the exuberance of the vernacular from their indie pop music and are puzzled why so few of our composers and writers get attracted to it.

Dominic Muldowney

USURY

The people are in debt,

they owe money.

Most nations are in debt,

they owe money.

Our banks are all in debt,

they owe money.

There’s just one thing

seems odd and funny,

exactly who is owed this money?

THE LUCIFER PARTY MANIFESTO

PUTTING LOCAL PEOPLE FIRST

It's time to talk to you from the heart. The credit crunch, social breakdown, political corruption, the drugs epidemic and the environment have all taken a terrible toll on our lives. It's easy, I know, to blame the previous government for mismanaging existence but we are all in this mess together.

Here at the Lucifer Party we offer a ray of hope. With our new Manifesto we will bring illumination to those problem areas created by the previous establishment's centralisation of power. In contrast the Lucifer Party is a broad party, a party of consensus and inclusion and as such I am pleased to tell you we have reached accord with Old Nick and his followers. Together we stand as the Co-Damnation.

But let me begin by bringing you good news: An election is coming and I want you to consider voting for radical change. Voting for a leader who is charismatic yet who isn't afraid to upset the status quo. And that is why I would like to put myself forward as the new candidate.

We at the Lucifer Party believe that it is time for a fundamental shift of power from gods to people. We want to promote decentralisation and democratic engagement, and put an end to the Judaeo-Christian era of top-down commandments by giving new powers to local councils, communities, neighbourhoods and individuals…

TWILIGHT SPEAKS

Twilight speaks with daily headline news
as armies, and religions on the move
increase but not in peace. The fulcrum slips
as epochs turn – the viruses mutate
and politicians lie through rictus grins
promising a cure of empty faith.

The nations' banks are minting fairy gold.
The Chancellor is ironing out the crunch
with made up figures that he hopes we'll buy.
Inside the vaults the assets fade to dust
and still the bankers hold out for a rise.
Your money's safest down the sofa's cracks
where pennies breed to pay your future bills
like barrows full of German marks for bread
as strikes and cries of "charity at home"
begin with calls for jobs for British folk.
The ups and downs of history cycle round.

and those on pensions pray the winter's mild.

Professor Dawkins rules us in his thoughts:
the truth, you'll find, is written in a code
it is the language of the universe:
the iron in your blood was synthesised
within the dying hearts of distant stars
and selfish genes determine who you are.
By definition you are just machine
searching for a maker in its dreams:
a simple programme dreaming it's alive.

At home the bible is the TV guide
a sacred text a modern oracle
that tells the times of your electric shrine
where love and war are digitally revealed
and entertained with tabloid sex and drugs
the mob cries out and glories in blood's trace.

Beneath the starry light a hooker smiles.

In silhouette her pimp is smoking crack,
the fissures in his eyes have caught the moon.
Summer cannot come for him, nor fall,
nor hope of spring - he lives in winter light
a minor detail in the patterns weave.
"Come and get a little high with me,
come and share some warmth within the dark
come and play the purpose of your life.
The brothel in your body and your blood
is waiting for the Madame in my mind."

The ghost of laughter whispers through the wreck.
And somewhere in the freezing depths of space
a dragon sperm is hurtling through the night:
an ancient rock of chemicals and ice
to fertilise this egg and start again
where money and the quest for fame have gone.

Time turned out beyond all memory.

THE ROMAN SONG

City of transvestites,
transmitting mobile phone tones,
trading tunes across the room.
A sparkling coliseum,
museum-mausoleum.

A gladiator sharpens
patterns in his beard
as flashing eyes of hot desire
ricochet round Rome.

Priests in skirts and dresses
on Vespas scoot past ruins,
running late to vespers
and traffic lights wink sequined eyes
as engines roar a rhythm.

Ancient ways and viaducts

are aqueducts of fashion
and passion plays ‘til light rise
when satin beauty vampires
put sun shades on in mourning
as all along the Roman song
consists of techno lyres
trysting tunes across the rooms.

Mediaeval spires jostle for attention
and hope for special mention
with quattrocento frescoes,
repro Michelangelos
framed in crumbling gesso,
racing the renaissance.

Tourists sacking hostels,
locals in their brothels
the old gods live in bars once more
worshipped by transgendered whores.
Vandals and barbarians

pass catholic grammarians
stepping down the Spanish way;
the old world's news still fresh today.

Sacred geometrics,
designer anaesthetics,
a kaleidoscope swirl of boy meets girl
repeats the beats of years in thousand,
changing the tones but tracing the tune,
shooting tunes across Rome's rooms...
the never ending beat goes on
in synthesised baroque
that marks each second of the clock.

But witty innuendo
gets a city in the end though.

So dress it up or dress it down
it's still the same eternal town.

THE HOUSE OF THE FURIES.

The conman comes
cascading cocaine fairy tales.
His words are powder,
his breath is powder
dribbling lies:

"Come shop with me in Oxford Street,
don't pay a thing, we'll nick the gear
and trade it on by trick or treat.

Debit and credit
are words that we can edit."

A drink, a wink, no time to think
and in a blink you're out of sync.

The Terror has come.

Madame Defarge in Westwood skirts
knits brittle little lies
which circulate the night
with photocopied wisdom.

In the rooms the women come and go
and talk of Maxine's menstrual flow.

The walls are paint effects,
they are not really here.
This is quantum space.

It is not here, it is not there,
it is not on the curving stair
of carnival creation.

If you eat the painted cakes
    (mirror, mirror on the wall,)
you swallow hunger

If you reach out for a friend
    (who's the alien at the ball?)
you'll kiss a stranger.

Here is danger.

Will ye steal, murder, and commit adultery,
and swear falsely, and burn incense unto Baal,
and walk after other gods whom ye know not;
and come and stand before me in this house,
which is called by my name, and say,
We are delivered to do all these abominations?

Oh yes we will,
we'll even kill.

We will shit on your name

We have no boundaries

We have no

We have

We...

Oxblood whispers,
on which are hung the copies of a phrase,
form a libel made of rage.
this place plays ritual on a loop
when the shaman is long gone.

I do not think he'll come again.

These acolytes, they will not wait
but play the palimpsest by eight
rewriting it with haste and hate.
while shitting on your name.

They say he's alcoholic,

they say he’s long gone bad,
they say he’s twisted, sick and evil.
A pass the parcel game.

Shall I arrange a little accident?
Shall I knock him off his bike?
Shall I greet him in an alley
with a smiling switchblade spike?

Their purpose has no centre
yet round and round they go
and talk of reputations
but never Michelangelo.

OBSERVER

The drinks industry is planning a ruthless campaign
The Observer can reveal.

Grape and grain.

On the streets of binge Britain
Britain keeps getting out of its brain.

'Vertical drinking' in vast neon drinking halls, earns
bonuses
a litany of tricks and sharp practice to maximise profits

Saturday night, in Basingstoke
a manager said we make people binge drink:
the more people drink, the more profits rise.
after four drinks they're 'captured' - you can tell by
their eyes.

Drunk and happy on cheap vodkatinis
A couple of lines and some ecstacy.
Drunk and happy on cheap vodkatinis
but ecstacy's still cheaper.

A little while later reports of a random attack.
In the center of town down by the War heroes' plaque.

Not including two stab wounds,
pissing in doorways, shouting abuse,
this is the first assault of the night.

Grape and grain and their juice.

"This bloke came from nowhere
and busted a fuse
said he'd rip off my face,
then he bit off my nose."

9 or 10 pints. Bring on the booze.

The middle-aged woman sprawled in the street,
in a little black dress and perilous heels,
will have some headache when she wakes.

She'll deny it was the booze of course.

How would she respond to the government
which says her behaviour is dangerous?

She leans forward and shouts at my notebook:

“I would say fuck off.”

CITY WHIRLPOOL

I sin.

I'm seduced by a lie from the past,

from the very first bricks of the very first city:

I'm seduced like the others,

drawn by the energy,

drawn by the promise, the paths and the pitfalls,

drawn to the magnet of mystic adventure,

drawn to a lie, on the run from a lie.

I've caught the momentum

that orbits the city.

Sucked in a whirlpool

and spun to the centre.

I've sacrificed my dreams

on altars of artifice,

prayed to strange djinn,

Position and Fame,

where value means money,
and failure's judged
as the ultimate shame.

And I've grinned as I've sinned
with drugs of remembrance,
persuading myself I see through the traps,
conspiring despite this with the ways of the city,
saying one day I'll turn back...

...perhaps...

And I search for forgiveness
in each new sensation
that draws me away
from the path I'm forgetting
and I'm lost even further
learning the mantra
whose bass wavelength hums:

it's pointless regretting...

Sooner than later
I forget that I'm sinning
and I blend with the colours,
fluorescent and twinkling
and I'm spun to the centre
no longer resisting,
with smiles giving into
this circus top spinning.

DYSTOPIA DRIVE

Slabs of concrete punctuate the night
as orange lamplight mitigates the grey.
No remembrance of those wine dark seas,
just sodden, wine-dark dreams haunt drinkers' nights
who, in their slumbers toss and face new fiends.
with turbulence and angst in twisted sheets,
and so embalmed in drink they grope for day
when reason reigns and sunlight guards the heart.

Some fantasise and daydream of great wealth
and pray for fame to vindicate their lives,
holding back the day when age will come,
an exile in some grim, grey old folk's home:
an opiated end of slow decay
where cool and careless, as he medicates,
Death wears a nurse's uniform, to blend.
A final friend of tranquilising smiles.

By day your coffin made from mortgaged walls
seemed better value than a quest for life
and mirrored in the fiction on TV
your brain is washed in liquid crystal tales
more weird and dreary than mere morphine dreams
as papers tell a narrative of knives
and youthful promise cut down in its prime.

You think it's safer than real life outside,
safer than the choice to live and yet
your life is just a chorus in the wings.
and so the show goes on, a perjury:
a story of two thousand years of lies.

MAD OLIVE

She'd seen it all,
she'd well divined the values of the future
but hadn't thought
the future would present itself so soon.

She despised the synthetic morals
they'd shaped from the wreck of a religion.

In the world, not of it.
This was the way she chose to be;
half Sybil, half challenge
to a tolerance that was pretended.

The last country wise woman
in London's village city;
she lived without the luxuries
all western children take for granted.
No running water, gas, no electric light

and visits to the doctor a distant memory:
She'd been strong,
defying each illness that approached.

She stared them out.

No one understood
the twin and run down houses
she had in the street.

All they thought was of their value,
how she could

"Sell… and live in comfort?"

All they thought was how they bruised their street,
detracting from the gentry look,
a selfish thorn that scratched at their profit.

Thousands of pounds

fractured their stucco,
thousands of pounds
they felt she denied them.

And soon all the newly moved
in guise of care, concern,
poked the council behind her back
behind their masks of friendship,
threatening her with the comfort
of a cosy old folk's home.

They pat her like a dog
in their Daily Mail approval:

> "She's quite eccentric
> been here for years, a character...
> we'd like to have her round for tea
> but she might become attached, I fear."

But she knows, she knows.

She knows the thoughts in embryo,
the words omitted as they mouth their goodness.
It doesn't fool her for a moment.

She is the tolerant one,
She fits in with, prostitutes herself
to the self admiration,
the smug satisfaction
their eyes cannot disguise.

When they talk of Olive
with their loving resignation,
they talk as if she were a child,
who's mentally impaired.

She knows that when they say

"Dear mad Olive, a character,
don't get on her bad side
(She's a little wilful)"

She knows what they mean is this:

> "Her houses are filthy
> and lower the tone of the street,
> they encourage drunks and squatters.
> Have you seen her teeth
> or smelt the urine
> and heard the curses,
> bad language and curses
> she throws if you upset her?
> She's a sensitive soul,
> a filthy, selfish sensitive soul"

She let's them say this
because she knows she is their mirror
and the person they describe
is their own reflection.

LOST PROPERTY

You couldn't sleep on this park bench
in London's neon, chemical rain.

Not here if you were lost, cold and drunk,
not here if your life was a walking madness,
not here if your stomach nerves ached with pain
at the thought of a life as a film passed by.

Could you lose yourself here, into the wood
that cradles a cracked old mould bony body?

But when in the day, low summer let's say,
the teen-twenty young explore with their hands
exchanging the bonds that might turn into bands,
do you think that their love is a comfort to him
or her or the kids that sleep here in winter?

Do you think that their life brings a smile to the man

that lies on this bed, on past life long dead
remembering something, of thoughts he once had?

But try to reflect that each tramp that lies here
carries his past in the beer on his breath.

THE DOGGING SONG

They say that cocaine
is becoming a pain
and ecstasy such a bore:
acid and crack, hashish and smack
are really too much of a chore.

But now a craze is all ablaze
from London to Dundee;
for rich or for poor
though it's breaking the law
it's absolutely free.

Yes, everyone's a swinger baby,
in or out of town,
everyone's been at it lately,
white or beige or brown.

They're dogging and shagging,

simple everyone's gagging
to get out onto a heath
and though Clapham Common
is strictly for bottoms
somebody must be beneath.

There's footballers, hairdressers,
lady mud wrestlers
up for a peak or a poke,
there are harlots and hustlers
and even sheep rustlers
as well as your average bloke.

From the forests of Devon
to Buckingham's parks
they're having a prod and a peep
and in the valleys of Wales
the locals regale
tourists with tales of loose sheep.

You can watch from your cars
or swing under the stars
with one or with two or with three.
Be a voyeur fantastic
trussed up in elastic
this form of gymnastics is free
for couples consenting
to experimenting
under the shade of a tree.

By a dark and deep bush
you might fancy a push
under the moon's silver light,
there's no need to fake it
get totally naked
but watch it gets cold now at nights.

The young lad next door
or an out of work whore
who's keeping her hand in for fun,

oh you'll keep wanting more
and make new friends galore
and by accident sometimes a nun.

Yes everyone's swinging,
they are dogging and diddling
for drugs are so yesterday.
Sneak into the night,
there's no reason for fright
and no chat lines on mobiles to pay.

You might meet the vicar
or a tranny who's thicker,
a pop star, a judge or a nurse.
It's all indiscreet,
this moist body heat
and it isn't confined to this verse.

But when your fling has been flung
in Dawn's purplish red,

check your flies aren't undone

when you creep home to bed.

THE OLD TRAMP

The old tramp sits there in the rain,
his red-gold eyes stare vacantly
as water mats his beard still further:
John the Baptist come again.

He's baptised in his urine
and the filthy liquid from the skies
that soaks the old coat, loosely draped,
and the baggy trousers round his thighs.

Fed on fags ends, Superbrew,
the city has provided,
a park bench is his Jordan,
his disciples are divided.

"Get him off the streets."
The Herods of health proclaim.
Whilst the Minister in question

dances seven lies,
veiling him in shame.

But the old tramp's been through the world and back,
he knows all about I'm-all-right-Jack
and he'd rather stare through the cold and rain
than let a stranger rearrange his brain.

He's waiting for his Christ
and his vacant look has purpose,
to filter out the dross of life
in his case his Saviour passes by.

He's waiting for the time
he'll be the first to recognise,
be accepted and baptise
the one that is akin to him.

He'll wait though for a while.

Through seasons heat and chill,
even when he's thin and ill
and even when, still on streets,
he's soaked and cold and dying
he'll keep his watch.

His golden eyes stare purposely.

BABY P

Baby P Baby P,
His Mother's watching MTV.
She's dreaming of celebrity.

Baby P is crying out.
The TV drowns the screams and shouts.
The boyfriend was a lager lout.

And it seems nobody knew.
Social service had no clue.
Little child beat black and blue.

And at the trial his mother cried.
"It wasn't me, why would I lie
or torture him before he died?"

And every witness said he smiled
through broken bones and love reviled

they said he was a trusting child.

Baby P. Baby P.

INNER CITY INTERNATIONAL

Curious changelings exploring this maze
spew blasphemous words they don't understand
as invisible eyes telescopes down
instantly sensing a knife on the ground.
A boy falls clutching a shirt that weeps red:
A careless action has silenced his mouth,
he forgot respect for the bloods to the south.
No prayers for the dead, no requiem said
and just like in films thugs pass with a shrug
on their quest to get high on mind blowing drugs.

Ziggurats menace the atmosphere's bounds,
minarets calling those faithful to greed,
temples of commerce where men worship gold,
high priests of money's perennial creed.
Bag-ladies, whose life is carried in hand,
look up where the rich drink vintage champagnes,
their smooth skins preserved through animal's pain

and shots of gene altered embryo glands.
Mink wrapped medusas with long polished claws
warily walk past the street corner whores.

Men armed in leather stalk streets in hunger ~
predatory eyes devour passers-by:
In darkness or daylight always the need,
raping the angels and stifling their cries.
Lords of the night club wink luminous eyes,
it's party time twilight and out come the freaks,
transparent and thin – they've not slept in weeks
living off moon juice and bright starry skies.
And no one is shocked that lives in this place:
you keep your mind by averting your face.

IT WAS HER SHOES

It was her shoes.

As she lay on the pavement,
gasping for breath
like a turtle on its back
her life unravelled;

She had fallen on the way to the estate,
to the towers and the keeps
of the castles of Roehampton.

Perhaps she had fallen many times before.

Her clothes, cheap and practical,
but her shoes were the shoes
of a proud, handsome woman.

Glossy black shoes, with a three-inch heel,

and a small satin bow
naughtily perched on the Oxford cap toe.

The shoes of a woman with money,
the shoes of a Lady in 1980.

Everything else was resigned
to the concrete turrets of the council's castles.

Her shoes had let her down by the crossing.

In the end her shoes had been her downfall.

ORACLE

The masked dancers are reading the changes
written on the walls of the labyrinth.

Another life reveals itself within the script,
another way is written on the walls,
on the streets and in the eyes of the unbelievers.

This new life has a different voice,
speaks and spreads joy as it wars in our minds.

This is the metal moment when we part from the past,
embrace new languages and articulate the fear
from the father's side.

This is the moment we decide
and read new identities into the fabric of the labyrinth
where the great beast is licking his chops
to illustrate a story where the monster's overcome

scarred by punctuation
from the mother's side.

New blossoms grow at the street corners,
where the labyrinth gives way to other times,
facing the east and hoping for a garden,
forcing their roots between the cracks in the old dressed
    stone
whose foundations were built on other labyrinths
when they were weeds,
which is just another name for wild.

This is the country of the past,
a tourist destination in period clothes and proper diction
where each colludes and everyone pretends the horror
    is not real
and stifles children's cries.

The country of the future has no walls
for there is no place left to hide the obvious

when the Minotaur's released,
smacking its chops as the new flowers bloom.

CLEANING UP POLITICS

VALUE FOR THE TAXPAYER

We have a wide-ranging programme to improve the political system we inherited from God. We are bringing forward reforms which aim to restore people's faith in their politics and politicians. We want our political system to be more accountable and more transparent.

With the Lucifer Party in control, life will take a different turn. We will bring a more caring, more just society, a society full of promise and not just promises. I will bring diversity yet be uniform, tough yet gentle, invest in important projects and make cuts where necessary, we must uphold the status quo but also make way for change. I offer you the voter real choice in morality, euthanasia and sex education for the under fives.

We believe that there are too many obstacles to social mobility and equal opportunities in the world today. Far too many young children are held back because of their gender, race, religion or sexuality. Clearly it is time to take positive action on this score. Therefore we will reflect this diversity in the make up of our party. And so I would like to introduce you to those members of our shadow cabinet the press have dubbed Lucifer's Lovelies...

WAY OUT

When goodness is lost
the people invent religion.

When religion dies
society invents morality.

When morality decays
the politician rises.

Then chaos comes.

THE POLITICIAN'S SONG

I'm a politician
and I've got a mission:
to educate the masses
working, mid and upper classes
and I maintain my power
through clever lies
which you devour
when I'm speaking on television.

So please don't think me sinister
I'm just an average minister
though do as I say
and not as I do.
No please don't think me sinister
I'm just an average minister
I'll have my way.
It's better for you.

I uphold old values
which on occasion I abuse
but my job is full of stress
so sometimes I wear a dress -
though the voters do not know
it's tame compared to some
whose names I keep on folio
in case I am accused.

I'm just an average minister,
for your good I administer
the nation's health
although it's not mine.
So please don't think me sinister
I'm just your average minister
and all of my wealth's
from corruption and crime.

You can pay for all my housing,
all my porn and my carousing,

I couldn't give a fuck

blame the banks, they're even worse.

Yes, it's time to pass the buck.

I find power so arousing.

I'm counting on a peerage

I might buy for it's a queer age

for I would sell my granny

drop my tryst with my wife's nanny

to keep my prospects glowing

my position and my pension.

For the EU, did I mention,

is where I will be going

where the gravy is still flowing.

Suits me right down to the ground.

There's nothing really sinister

about this average minister

although I vote for war
I live life above the law
it's part of my life's mission.

I'm doing what I feel like
yet seeming quite sincere
when I walk up to the mike
and speak on television.

RADOVAN KARADZIC

War crimes suspect Karadzic
enjoyed his summer breaks
among the very people that
it's said he sought to kill.

The mastermind behind mass murder
of Muslims, ethnic Croats,
was on a bus from Serbia bound
for some seaside sun.

Seven men got on and said
they were the secret service.
They went straight up to this old man
who calmly read his book.

One shouted please remove your beard,
then grabbed and yanked it hard.
Karadzic cried out in pain

(For it was his own).

The agent said: "We've followed you
for 15 days, what's more
we know all your secrets now.
You won't escape again."

POWER

Let's shout at the familiar,
formal way of the hypocrite.
The hiding place of prudes,
a double-standard favourite.

Let's laugh at the self-proclaimed,
dissembling bigot's public face;
condemning pleasures he desires
whilst calling it a great disgrace.

Let's see how power's siren scent
twists its opposition
with sycophantic gilded fluff.
Behold, the politician.

THE DAO OF POWER SONG

I come in peace.
I'll leave you in pieces.

Wash in me, I won't leave creases.
I'm the journey not the destination,
value for money low inflation
electric highway information.

I'm chairman miaow
riding the Dao
to take you to heaven
with a big fat spliff.

I'm the magnificent seven
riding high on 9/11.

You're hearing but you do not learn.
You listen but you do not hear.

Truth is not your true concern.
You look for me in pints of beer.

I come from a future that is not yours
no smack, no crack no neon doors.

I'm the man who can,
I'm the quick fit fitter
I carry the can
but I'm not bitter.

I ain't heavy, I'm your Big Brother,
Keeping watch, just like Mother,
Email snooping tabloid thrill,
007 license to kill.

I'm detox, botox, sugar free
decaffeinated herbal tea.
You won't believe that I'm not butter
but in the end I'll cure your stutter

I'm a hit, wit, strawberry split
I'm definite and infinite.
I'm a bluey white
I'm lemony fresh
I'm the stars at night
and sunlight made flesh.

I reduce the appearance of fine lines.
I am the last of the summer wine.

I'll quote you happy,
be a cheeky chappie,
I'm a comfy, no leak disposable nappy,
I'm a Werther's original,
I'm tampax smooth,
I'm the greatest hits,
I am rare groove.

I'm a mass distraction in a wonderbra,
I'm High on flavour low on tar,

I'm 0% finance
on a brand new car,
the bank that said yes
to a trendy wine bar,
star for a night, the price is right
Pepsi Max and Miller Lite.

I'm a footballer's wife
going under the knife,
the politicians smiling lie
surveillance from the 'Eye in the Sky.'

I'll do it anyway, smell the fear.

I'm a celebrity?
Get me out of here...

HUMAN CATTLE

Where you see human cattle
ripe for digital branding
and chip and pinning in their pens,
I see individuals
living lives as best they can.

But you, my corporate friend,
see farm animals.

Where you see sources for experiments,
testing chemicals to turn a profit,
your public think you care
and have the interest of their lives at heart.

Because you play a game of numbers
where humans cease to be
becoming 'things' instead.

And that puts you outside of life.

Which is unforgivable.

SOMEBODY ELSE

Just look at them on TV.
They haven't a clue
what's really going on.
From the PM to local MP
somebody else is pulling their strings.

Look at their eyes
filled with a fire
not wholly their own,
the defensive mouth,
the shit-eating grin.

Somebody else is pulling the strings.
Someone with horns and leathery wings.

ELIZABETH THE LAST

It's a bust of Elizabeth the Last,
the MP said, part of a new series
commissioned to commemorate the past
and put a stop to all those queries
on why we put an end to rule by kings and queens
with properly elected political has-beens.

It's made from real resin and its eyes,
I hope, have captured the cold and steely gaze
of one who never seemed to like surprise,
who liked to keep the status quo unfazed.
It's funny when you think Camilla almost brought them down
with images of her in fluffy mules, a negligee and crown.

They had a national church back then you know...
I thought to sculpt them too, but now who cares?

And York and Canterbury? They had to go.
And to your right's the bust of Tony Blair.
Thanks to him we're fixed within the Presidential
    scheme
and constitutional monarchy is just a distant dream...

HOUSE OF LORDS

When I am old and worthy
and elected to the Lords
I shall buy some half moon glasses
and attend the house by Internet
from my summer house abroad.

I shall head the new committees
and peer through half moon specs
at waitresses in restaurants
and buxom girls that show their sex.

I shall educate the masses
and intimidate the lower classes.
And with grand deliberation
I'll keep my job
as chief panjandrum of the nation.

MURDER 1899 (A PHOTOGRAPH)

A sepia Christ
blasts through the years.

Trial by press
and the pale mob's threat
that Justice must be seen and done?

It's still a lynching
electrically disguised.

Pale hands pretend
it's science
makes them check the straps
and feel the leather.

The local brass
dressed up for the camera
recording their magnificence

at the *nigger's* execution.

A hundred years later
this frightening picture,
cruel and anonymous,
speaks to me.

It cuts through my laughter,
my confident smile
that everything's fine,
that all's for the best,
that weighing it up,
government knows.

When I look at the man
he's in a foreign land
bearing the burden
and truth in his eyes
where words become
the skin of thought.

HEALTHY LIVING AND RECREATION

IMPROVING LOCAL LEISURE SERVICES

Whilst The Lucifer Party, as the only real choice in liberal fundamentalism, is clearly against prohibition we believe it is only right that you manage your addictions in a responsible and tax effective manner. Therefore we have decided to:

- Ban the sale of alcohol at below the price of duty plus vat to address binge drinking.
- Tackle binge drinking without unfairly penalising responsible addicts, pubs and important local industries such as casinos and the Hellfire Club.
- Double the fines on premises selling alcohol to the under-fives and to allow councils and the police to shut down permanently any shop or bar that persistently sells alcohol to toddlers unless accompanied by a teenager.

We will also introduce powders to counteract 'legal highs' to better protect vulnerable young people.

Whilst the opposition and the right wing press have unfairly smeared our leader Mr Dave Lucifer as the 'original dealer', we feel this is unfair and taken out of context. Mr Lucifer would like to make it clear that during his time at the Garden of Eden PLC he was merely conducting botanical studies of the psychogenic properties of the local flora as part of his internship. His offer to the gardener's wife of the fruit in question was an entirely innocent and typically considerate gesture misconstrued by Ms Eve Human. He was completely unaware that the CEO had in fact genetically engineered the fruit to expand consciousness. After an internal enquiry Mr Lucifer was cleared and both Eve and her gardening partner Mr Adam Human were asked to leave by security and an injunction was taken out preventing them from coming within a lifetime of Eden PLC.

We will also be taking steps to update the outdated honours system to reflect society as it is today. The C.B.E will now be replaced by the C.F.E or Chav From the Estate and a new honour will shortly be announced: The C.O.M or Celebrity on the Make.

We will also be tightening up regulation on tightening up so that haemorrhoid creams can no longer be sold as instant face lift in a jar unless it also contains at least 25% micro-fabulisers...

PEACH SCHNAPPS

Last night Peaches
received mouth to mouth
close sources said.
Her drug overdose
has led to concern.

According to reports.

"Peaches is out of control."
Say her friends:
"Peaches is losing the plot."

Her Mother died of an overdose.
Friends worry she's forgot.

Peaches collapsed at home.
A friend gave the kiss of life.
Thank God she wasn't alone.

She looked stunning last night
at the premiere
in Leicester square.

According to reports.

Speaking to the London paper
after she was out of danger
Peaches launched an attack:

“Everyone prejudges me
I think that’s unfair.”

Her father makes her stick to a curfew
but she’s nineteen going on twenty:

“My father lives in Battersea
but I live in King’s Cross
He cannot lock me in each night.”

According to reports.

Her father says he'll go ballistic
if Peaches turns to drugs.

Her mother's view was fatalistic.

According to reports.

A spokesman said
"Its business as usual
Peaches is quite in control."
dismissing the rumours out of hand.

According to reports.

FAME

So desperate to create an impression
the starlight screamed;
no longer himself – the real sun – he became a
singularity
into which he grabbed impressions of other lives
pulling an identity out of its socket
and plugging it into the holes in his psyche.

So desperate to become a light
he extinguished himself in his emotions,
springing leaks throughout his psychosphere:
wounds of self created agonies
born from old despairs, frustrations and sense of
isolation
consuming himself, fat with anger
that fuelled the need to shine.

He became a dim and distant star

that none could touch;
outside the galaxy of other lights,
the family of brightness that danced together,
refusing its pull to join the dance.

And so it became a pole star
an aid to navigation
that other lights might see
and steer their path from.

DEATH OF AN ACTOR

I saw death steal upon him
with a shadow.

He was old in an old folk's home
He'd been known for being
sometimes bitter, rude
and sometimes crude.

It had been said to him

"When you clear a room,
don't make enemies dear!"

But he'd been a lackey,
a secondary character
in someone else's play.

And though he said

that he was seventy,

he was eighty,

and when he said,

I'm getting to eighty,

you knew a century was a wink away.

He lived in an old people's home

for retired theatricals and a change came about him.

He didn't struggle against death,

death took him on an old fashioned tango and foxtrot

and played and danced with him

and his ways became gentle

and he became soft and subtle.

And in all his hallucinations

there was a twinkle in his eye

and a smile that made you realise

he had changed.

And as he diminished he didn't rant,

he didn't fight and try
to force his ego on the world,
his personality had become
so unimportant.

He smiled and sat in the sun
amongst the parakeets
and the pantomime horses of his mind
beside the goldfish pond at the home,
the old people's home for old theatricals.

You were always greeted at the door
by a silent-movie star who said
"welcome to my Country House.
How nice of you to come."
And he smiling at it all,
allowing her it all
winked you in to the chaos and fun.

The bitchy queen

he'd been was gone,
he was mellow and prepared for death,
and death teased, tricked and flirted
and death blessed him and kissed him
on his forehead from time to time
and they laughed knowingly at each other
in their private little game.

And so he slipped for a while
from this strange world
and he slipped a little further each time I saw him
until he was just a radiant white-haired smiling saint
quite aware, though the doctors might have said
    otherwise,
quite aware, though the doctors might have felt
    otherwise,
he was quite aware.

Because amongst all his hallucinations
and his desire for the world he was in

there was always a grin and a smile
and after a while the hallucinations and dreams took
over
and moreover, he diminished
and yet he did not become some nodding bladder on a
stick
like so many that lived in the actor's home.
The old people's home for retired theatricals.

He smiled, his personality truly changed
as though finally he realised the truth of life
in the truth of death.

And it seemed that far from running from death
he waited for him,
waiting for his three minute call
as he took off the last of his make-up.
All the times he died on stage or film,
had prepared him for this moment.

He finally let go and he was there.

They found him in the morning,
death came at night,
a long awaited and secret admirer,
slipping perfectly to an obvious conclusion.

And although one can say
he was full of delusion at the end
(maybe it was the medication,
maybe it was preparation.)
he was happy and fulfilled and golden.

But I'll always remember him
in his graceful dance with death,
dignified, transfigured and courted at last
by a welcome, true and loyal lover.

B LIST

You can see the celebrity's
masked insincerities
and fear of it all
that glares from his eyes
that he hopes you won't see.

He's half disappointed
he got what he wanted
aware of the truth
that he's given his youth
with no more to be had.

He starts to despair
God answered his prayers
and he wishes he'd stretched them
that little bit higher
for something more lasting.

But at the club opening
he's started hoping
something or someone
will take him away
from the flashlight and fans.
He feels his hope drain
with each line of cocaine
and all he can muster
is a clenched facile grin
that could be mistaken
for feeling at home.

But no photos are taken,
he can't get attention
for another like him
has broken the surface
of fame's shallow waters
and he's stuck with the daughters
of loan sharks not pop stars.

THIS IS YOUR LIFE

"This is your life!"
The silver haired cut-out
smiles at the tramp.

"Born long ago,
origin unknown,
you've become quite a feature
of Capital sights.
You've characterised
an ageless tradition
in our London life…

Now for our first guest
here us your wife."

Toothless Bag lady
reels up to Trampy
pleased by the camera,

the lights and the crew.
She pulls from her bag
a couple of dog ends
and half a can of Superbrew.

"I've been called a witch,"
she slurs to his face,
"they've said nasty things
though I'm still human race
and I'd just like to say
Old Trampy, my love,
to your health you old sod
on this your great day.

Trampy's unsure
and lets off a fart,
snatches the lager
and downs it in part.

"Now for another

you thought was your brother.
Please welcome this man…"
Silver presenter
winks to the camera
as well overdressed
comes the next guest.
"…Here's City Gent."

A round of applause,
as pin striped and well fed
comes one of life's bores.

"Well I've known Old Trampy
from time immemorial,
and I have to say
(though I've been more than cordial)
he's been rather rude
though I always gave
from his birth to this grave
a little spare change

to buy him some food.

Plump City Gent
with his red polished face
shakes Trampy's hand
and retires to his place.

"Now for your friend."

At last thinks the old tramp,
we're nearing the end.

"Yes here to remind you
of fun you have had
is Mad Drunken Tom..."

(but viewers it's sad,
he's not here tonight
so up on the screen
is his accolade...)

There is his friend
on a hospital bed.
He can't quite hear
the message that's said
and he's unaware
that his friend is long dead.

The laughter dies down
and trampy turns round.
He lifts up his coat,
baring his arse,
and lets the world know
what he thinks of this farce.

THE BALLAD OF SUSAN AND GEORGIE

When Susan met Georgie
and Georgie met Sue
they thought it was love
pure, vanilla and true.

They said *my moppet*, *my poppet*
and *my only* to top it
and even sometimes *coochy coo*.

But then Georgie and Susan
warm Sue and sweet Georgie,
found love not enough
that they wanted an orgy.

Soon they were wanking,
spanking and thanking
the Lord for the pleasures of sex.

They were fucking and sucking
and generally tucking
into delights of the flesh.

And they diddled and fiddled
with no pause in the middle,
tied up with yards of black flex.

They were stripping and whipping,
pill popping, coke sniffing
in a frenzy that went to their heads.

They had duos and trios
with increasing brio
manacled onto their beds

But sadly the story
of George and Sue's orgy
took a dire and terrible twist:

Sue was padlocked in chains
and George passed out in pain,
impaled on a huge plastic fist.

But then an idea
came, crystal clear:
With one final groan
her toe pushed the phone.

She dialled 999,
writhing and heaving,
but all that was heard
was deep, heavy breathing.

Soon flashing and whining
came fire fighters, nurses
cop car lights shining
and I'll skip the last verses…

Oh Susan, said Georgie,

I want love not an orgy,

it's been such a pain in the arse.

Oh Georgie, said Sue,

I agree with you too,

let's make love in the sun on the grass.

SEBASTIAN'S LAST WEDDING

You were late for your wedding.
Your bridesmaids were working girls
dressed up in their Friday best
for the venereal-funereal day.

This cortege in corsets
followed the whores-drawn crystal jewel,
marking this time with sobs
and poses for the News of the World.

They'd lost their best punter:
a real gent and toff who
knew how to treat a lady
mad on crack.

You were a beautiful bride
dressed up in hot red sparkles,
Marc Bolan sang with *sturm und drang*

of a twentieth century boy
but the song was wrong:
you were an 1890s dandy from the 1980s.

You were the secret lovechild
of Marilyn Munroe and Sid Vicious
with shades of Baudelaire and Wilde.

You were delicious and delightful,
frightful, terror-shy and gentle,
fanny-friendly, gay and stately.

As your jeweled, wooden wedding dress,
in hot pink spangles, arrived at the altar,
Death arrived in silent splendour
and made an honest woman out of you at last.

FANCY A LINE?

Fancy a line?

It's made from powdered blood
mingled with shit;
a condom bursting
in a smuggler's gut.

And the smile of your dealer,
(that kind, trusted friend)
hides a trail of betrayal,
of enslavement, despair.

And the hit of the coke
is the thrill of a murder,
the high of a hitman
in drug war vendetta.

And the ghost in your head

that breathes paranoia,
is the voice of the dead
who have died for your fix.

And soon as you bloat
drinking deep for some silence
there's a struggling thought
you're a murderer too.

So get out the blade
and chop up a line.
Go on. Rack it up:
I can see you're dying for it.

POSESSION IS NINE TENTHS OF THE LAW

Poor junkie you're possessed.
There's a screaming lobster boiling in your mind
that you silence with excess.

The bad times were fun with the underclasses.
You wore sunglasses and never understood
why the sun was always dark.

Deluded alchemist,
searching everywhere except the world around you
pursuing your identity
in cooked up kitchen chemistry.

You'll wear yourself threadbare,

THE COSMETICALLY CORRECT SONG

If you're low on self respect
and you want to be cosmetically correct,
you must copy the stars,
be a Venus, with scars
and hope that your friends won't suspect.

As the muse of Da Vinci once said:
try smiling when going to bed,
nature knows nought
and looks can be bought
for even the plainest get wed

So, learn to tease like Mona Lisa,
keep them guessing when you smile.
Fake and take's the name of the game
use a little guile.

Short legs - wear stilettos,

big shoulders - wear high necks
no curves in your silhouetto
pad them out like the rest.

Short and dumpy? Get a hat,
black's good if you are fat.
Too tall? - learn to slouch.
Head held high, don't be a grouch.

Camouflage and misdirect
as you polish up your self-respect,
learn to tease like Mona Lisa
and be cosmetically correct.

Creams can smooth a flaky skin,
learn to slink if you are thin.
Got no lips? Just paint them in
or pump them full of collagen.

If your breasts are minimum

fill them up with silicone.
If keeping fit is much too drab
they can suck out all your flab.

You could always try it,
the latest new-fad-diet,
or bran and prunes and salad and cabbage
as much as you can manage

Camouflage and misdirect
as you polish up your self-respect,
learn to tease like Mona Lisa
and be cosmetically correct.

MR DOHERTY'S DILEMMA

For the madness in my blood
I spilled my cup
with lunacaemic paranoia.

I liked Goya
not Michelangelo.

Don't fuck with me
I'm Caravaggio
tormented by Dionysus
and sodium lamps
and up to no good.

For the moon's in my blood
and the moon's in my mind
and the moon's in my dance
and it shines in my eyes.

Cackling asides
in dim basement moth bars,
ketamine strides
in mercury fur
that gleams in the gutter
and rich lunar eyes
that are up to no good...

> Where the moon's in my blood
> and the moon's in my mind
> and the moon's in my dance
> and it shines in my eyes.

I am the lycanthrope,
a human kaleidoscope:
By day I'm a man,
but my lunacaemia,
the disease of my clan,
opens up a different world
where I'm up to no good...

With the moon in my blood
and the moon in my mind
when I'm up for the madness
that shines in my eyes.

THE SABOTEUR WITHIN

The saboteur within
feeds on contradiction,
he fears the way towards success
whilst writhing with ambition.

The saboteur within
won't learn and take advice
stays out late on pills and booze
and pays dawn's fragile, working price.

The saboteur within
feeds upon frustration,
a red faced, angry, crying child
amidst the wastes of his creation.

Resist the saboteur within
in case you fail where you would win.

PARTY PEOPLE

Party people, party people,
always shining, hearty people;
pop a trippy smarty people.

Party friends, party friends,
sometimes smiley, party friends;
beat and music never ends.

Night time people, people tall,
cross dressed people, people small;
wide eyed grins don't sleep at all.

Lots of movement, never still,
another snort, more time to kill.
Party people getting ill.

Party friends who never work.
At thirty eight they've gone berserk.

In therapy they do woodwork.

Party people slowing down
in sheltered housing out of town,
dancing in their dressing gowns.

Party friends aren't hard to find;
they'll gladly help you spend your mind.

MODERN DREAMS AND DILLEMAS

I could have been a football hero,

but what about my books?

I could have been a scholar,

but what about my looks?

I might have been a rock star baby,

though what about my god?

Maybe been a dedicated priest

but I'm probably too odd.

I wanted to climb mountains,

but I like to watch TV.

Or maybe been a film star

except it's solitude I seek.

I could have been a doctor,

though people make me sick.

Or been a tabloid writer

but I can't throw mud that sticks.

A dilletante's not too bad
but I like to do one thing:
I'll be a modern artist
write, paint and act and sing.

You should have been a football hero.

BYRON

Late April, Missolonghi.
His revolution was dead in its tracks,
the Turks skulking at the back of his mind.

He watched the miming
of doctors unable
to massage his life
whilst draining him dead.

He turned his head.

Charlatans...

His contempt was tempered
with bone-deep exhaustion:
Veins opened, flesh studded with leeches,
too drained of life to stop them
drawing pints of his blood,

covered with leeches.

His melody missed tones,
his song was out of tune.

Did they suppose I wished for life?

What could be said?
Pretending their quackery
could save one much worsened
by medical fakery,
the disciplined panic
they tried to conceal
in kindly murderous eyes,
eyes not meeting the dying truth,
silent, manic at their impotence.

Lies, just lies.

The ghost of a belly laugh ripped through his ruin.

My truth... he murmured.

The doctors, busy
summoning the dark.

My poor dear Ada...

His daughter's name escaped its prison
at the thought and the image
of another life - home.

Sliding between his sweat,
he slipped down the darkness
and stretched its meniscus

That within me tires,
Torture and Time
in each breath I expire.

The cavalry charge was galloping wildly,

the cavalry purchased
with fame, pleas and money
galloping through the stage of his mind,
galloping with each beat of his pulse.

No more! They saw his lips move.

His eye-light receded
with conscious surrender,
not struggling, not quiet,
waiting, anticipating,
anxiety fading
as he recognised this was a friend.

LOips slumped in smile.

At that moment the sky exploded
strobing the night with a vomit of rain
as the blink of white clarity
light flashed the poet,

expressing the moment.
catching the void
in his eyes glassy opals.

The whisper crescendoed,
bursting cascades, rippling words,
flooding the space of his hopers
spreading through Greece,
tapping on Europe.

The great man is gone.

And the god's he had fought for
teased, tricked and kissed him,
gods long suspected
welcomed him home.

OLD ROCKERS

That's how old rockers go,
they ride their quad bikes into the night,
the drink and drugs behind them
and old enough to know
they're too old for a fight.

Fifty nine approaching they leather up,
kick off, accelerate into the wind
their pony tails stick out their helmet,
a Roman knight, wide eyed grins.

They charge into the final battle,
Valiant. Their greatest hits
playing in their ears.

That's how old rockers go:
their mark well made upon the years.

WASTRELS HAVE KNOWN

Wastrels have known, they always know it
though they might not care to show it.
Perhaps they see too much of mind
perhaps it is the rest that's blind
who leave the child within behind.

Wastrels know that they have blown it
though they might not care to own it.
When others pass their promise by
embracing culture's stately lie,
they keep their minds intact thereby.

Through drugs they've lost their sense of profit
they can't seem to keep quite off it.
They've seen the scene and how it is
and won't adopt the Judas kiss.
They see, they see it how it is.

Wastrels know. They've always known it.
In Greatness' shadow they have flown it
with Pablo, Ernest and with Lorca
they've flown from Cuba to Majorca
and lived on high as beat New Yorkers.

And if you'd care to ask a tramp,
piss-baptised beneath street-lamps,
he'd tell his life and how he'd known it,
and how he knew he'd never owned it,
and how it's been since he's blown it.

And just so you know - wastrels know
you know too, but just won't own it.

DIVERSITY AND TOLERANCE

THE IMPORTANCE OF FAITH IN LIFE TODAY

(From the blog of Mr. Dave Lucifer*)

It's been a divine week on the campaign trail. First, I attended Eid-ul-Fitr. Last night I broke bread with the Chief Rabbi, who has just marked the Jewish New Year and today I am delighted to be dining with the Bishops of the Church of England. And on Friday I will be meeting His Holiness the Pope for an ecumenical black mass.

So if anyone suggests that our party has no interest in people of faith, or even dare I even say, does not "do God", then I hope my schedule this week will go some way to banishing that myth.

But to be serious, I think everyone here will agree that we have had a big problem in the world in the way God has been handling issues of faith and religion. I would even go further: and say we have a big problem in the way we think about faith in our society as a whole.

It was once said when people stop believing in God they believe in anything. But that is not strictly true, religion is just a supernatural form of politics; the voters become apathetic and we get a low turn out at election time. That is why I am urging you to listen to my manifesto for change and believe in me instead.

Today you say you're atheists but I know there's a nagging doubt among some of you who think to yourselves "What if I'm wrong?" The opposition will tell you they stand for morality. But how true is that really? If they really have a set of morals and ethics worth retaining, let us look at their work in the Middle East. Let us read the accounts of genocide, infanticide, murder and rape visited on the chosen and infidel alike. It's all set out in their previous manifestos, which you now call Holy Writ.

*with apologies to Baroness Warsi

SAMSON AND THE NEW WORLD ORDER

Do they dream of Samson
pushing at pillars
to topple the temples
in the Philistines metropolis?

Did Delilah offer coca cola
and breasts that bleed bullets
from Vietnam to Angola,
flaunting her dollars,
lap dancing an innocence
that she's not what she seems?

She is made from the dreams
in a bottle of djinn.

But Samson's been laden
with a terrible burden,
invoking the names

of the prophets of God
to justify war
on the armies of profit.

But what if this *god*
is a turbulent spirit
that's born from a darkness
that's scheming within?
And what if it's dreaming?

For the Philistines pray
to barbarous spirits
and the Philistines pay
for this barbarous power.

In a city of towers
false minarets
and bright neon spires
call all to obey what the dollar desires.

But there is another
from Afghanistan,
a Muslim saint, a holy man
whose death united
Sufis, Christians, pagans, Jews.

Rumi's dancing verse is suffused
with one word.

And that word is Love.

OPINION

The papers say they've got the bomb
to wipe their enemy from the earth.
"For God", the cry, raised on their streets:
the tension in the region rises
as blood runs high and ways are strange
these cold missiles are the new long range.

Tick tock - a clock, tock tick - a click
Tick tock - a clock, tock tick - a click

The War between a desert god
and science rages through the world.
for who shall rule men's minds at last ~
Blind faith or knowledge through the ages?
A dirty bomb to makes us pure
which even science cannot cure.

Tick tock - a clock, tock tick - a click

Tick tock - a clock, tock tick - a click

This god of peace that loves through hate
breeding darkness in kids' hearts:
where blood is good, it shows you love,
where limbs are torn praise rises up.
Just defending your beliefs
from the unbeliever thieves.

Tick tock - a clock, tock tick - a click
Tick tock - a clock, tock tick - a click

From God a bomb, for us a tomb
as rights turn wrong, a mushroom blooms

SIMILAR

If you heard the sound
of a baby's laughter,
could you tell the baby's colour?
If the laugh had gender?

Is this the sound
of a Muslim or a Jew?

Could you tell
if this sound of innocence
belonged to Us or Them?
Which is only me and you.

We are all brothers and sisters.

Just different shades
in a picture bigger than ourselves,
just pixels in the cosmic mind.

DARWIN OUR HELP

Darwin our help in ages past
redeem our foolish ways,
re-clothe us in our rightful mind
The Mail On Sunday says.

Professor Dawkins offers praise
to all our greatest thinkers
whose minds are free of mystery
and superstition's blinkers:

"There really is no need for faith
with knowledge on your side.
The theory of big bang is fact
and Genesis is lies.

For Science is the only source
of all free thinking logic,
belief in god is immature

I really thinks it's tragic.

Religion is illogical:
it's just belief in magic."

Our God who is the God of all.
must be allowed Its due.
Our sacred books must be obeyed
whether or not it's true

The Bishop gave his views today
and prayed for Dawkins' soul
and said that in a real sense
God's word is true and whole.

The Rabbi backed him up and said
"God's views are made quite clear,
Leviticus must be obeyed:
Transgression is severe."

The Imam took a different stance
and said the present war
between the West and True Belief
would lead to Sharia Law.

Freethinkers all must be suppressed
as we have done before.

MONOCHROMATISM

When you approach me
forgetting your race
I'm unaware of mine.

If I come to you
without my religion
don't turn yourself
into a shrine.

When you come along,
politics gone,
we talk about sports and our mates,
what we have in common,
the things that we share
and laugh with no need
to translate.

When we look to each other

as mirrors of self,

I forget I am white you are black.

If I greet you with smiles

don’t put me through trials,

we’re cousins,

no need for attack.

So come on, approach me

with all that you are.

The journey from you

into me isn’t far.

DRAMA

Give me petrol,
give me drama,
let me meet
the Dalai Lama.

Rope the Pope
he's no hope
when you want to
cure your karma.

Hang the bankers
causing chaos,
bloody wankers,
lying charmers.

Hate the State's
strangling weight,
storm the city
in pyjamas.

IT IS TIME

"It is time to stop the suffering and hate,"
said the prophet,
"it is time to look to humanity's survival.
It is time, it is time, though it's getting late."

"Just a minute," said the head of one nation
"When I've finished killing my enemies
I shall devote all my time to peace."

"I'll get around to it when I've dealt
with all the evil people." said a king.
"It's all very well," remarked the president
"but you don't have to make laws
with punishments to fit the crime,
when we've tinkered with society
and achieved some moral sobriety
then we can pause,
then there will be time."

And while they argued,
the prophet kept crying:
"it is time, it is time, it is time."
until he was old and grey.

And as the lords of this earth looked at him
they saw ranting senility and had him put away.

GOD IS NOT

God is not a Christian,
a Moslem or a Jew.
God has no religion,
not Buddhist or Hindu.

No way to It is better,
no way more blessed or true
than honouring the sacred
that lies in me and you.

God isn't black or white
God isn't gay or straight,
God doesn't have a gender:
Just Wisdom - never hate.

So when you meet a stranger
whose ways makes him seem... *other*,
remember, God is in him too
and that makes him your brother.

THE SUPPLICANT'S SONG

I saw a man talk rainbows
catching dragons in the air.
Much redder than the rose
his flaming hair,
such eyes of blue
the sky shone through.

He said:

No realms
for princes anymore,
no place for angels
or the sacred law.
No profit from
the prophets knocking on your door.

But you don't remember.

I just breathe in

and then I breathe out

once again,

I am the desert

and the pouring rain

bringing you laughter

and bringing you the pain.

Just so you remember.

He said:

From the most

microscopic living thing

to bursting suns

a million light years out in space

I surf the wavelength

of the tune

without a trace

and still I don’t remember.

Why isn’t god listening?
Why doesn’t he hear our anxious prayer?
Perhaps he’s gone fishing
or maybe he’s really just not there

So bring on the angels
the gurus and buddhas of this age.
We’ve all become strangers
we have forgotten how to pray.

Let’s try and remember.

NEW EDITION

God looked at his words;
sees too many adjectives.

It's time to edit.

GANGRENE

The Celestial stem
has worms in the meat
and the evil deeds of parents
come out in the child
in sorcery and miasma.

This is the curse of the ancestors

these are the ones who can

and the disease they send

these are the ones who want

for our neglect

these are the ones nobody can see.

The new seed sprouts,
things rot away
and new beginnings can be found
in the insects breeding
in fermenting fruit.

What does the rot breed?
    Life.

Where does the seed grow?
    Rot.

This is breathing
which brings about a healing of the times.

CARING FOR OUR ENVIRONMENT

A CLEANER GREENER TOMORROW

We believe we must protect the environment for future generations, make our economy more environmentally sustainable, and improve our quality of life and well-being. We also believe that much more needs to be done to support the farming industry, protect biodiversity and encourage sustainable food production.

We are therefore examining a series of measures to protect biodiversity and wildlife. We will deliver a new, ambitious biodiversity strategy for the next ten years. We will also create new Life System Designations, or LSD, to allow local people to protect the green spaces which are important to them. We are also improving these spaces through the creation of Nature Improvement Areas, supported by what sounds like an awful lot of money but on closer inspection will prove to be rather less I'm afraid. You get the picture.

Thanks to my encouragement in the fields of science and technology you have taken complete possession of your planet. But not entirely with happy consequences it is true. You've come a long way from your origins in Eden and now the Lucifer Party feels it is time for you to eat of the Tree of Life, which is the

Number One promise in our new all dancing, all singing manifesto. Once this has been achieved, the savings made in health care can be diverted into education. Once you realise you can live forever you might then begin to start taking slightly more care of your garden. Stop throwing your rubbish onto the lawn and start cultivating it with humility. This is not however part of the opposition's plan. The opposition wants to hold an Armageddon instead which is rather like trying to tidy up a mess with a nuclear bomb. Whereas we at Lucifer Central think you are not quite that stupid and would prefer it if you just got with the programme instead - Hmmn?

APOCALYPSE CALYPSO

This Eden is heating
degree by degree
the ice caps are melting away.

The green is retreating,
tree upon tree,
as everyone slowly turns gay…

Oh… the apocalypse calypso
is the latest dance in town
as the oil and gas reserves run out
and the earth beneath turns brown.

The apocalypse calypso
will be danced by every nation
as famine and disease ride in
to reduce the population.

The apocalypse calypso
will speed up evolution
when water sources can't be drunk
because of the pollution.

The apocalypse calypso
is Armageddon chic
it's living for the moment
when the outlook's rather bleak.

Oh the apocalypse calypso
is the only dance that's left
and you've only got yourselves to blame
for your global greed and theft.

LORD INDUSTRY

Lord Industry's no fool.
He knows what's going on:
he created it.

But behind the confidence,
charities and statistics
he's grown neurotic.

He'd always thought:

Science will discover
ways to decontaminate,
clean and disinfect
the progress I have made.

Now, he's not so sure.

Standing on the beach

with his granddaughter,
she asks him what the stench is
why the sea is oily?

He notices dead fish
deformed from birth
and feels the acid
rise from his stomach
as he recalls the restaurant
that specialises in seafood
and the meal he's just had.

His granddaughter looks at him
and sees behind the smile
the eyes are frozen.
so she squeezes his hand
innocently assuring him
that everything's just fine.

IT WOULD MEAN NO BLUEBELLS

I

The forests burn
to make the pretty lights
that shine in Vegas.

The Earth at night
consumed with city lights.
Lord save us.

War - the theme of rich men's dreams.

II

Give me all the old gods
to sacrifice the past.

Let religions burn
their funeral pyre

the future cannot last.
The future is a fire.

Let trees breath,
let the skies be clean,
the waters pure.

Find the cure.

So I'm praying to the prophets
and the buddhas come before us.

Help us wake up from this dream.

III
The shore is sick
with half digested
vomit of the sea.

A mist, appalled,
rolls in to hide
the ocean's scream
as sky sperm tourists
sunbathe by
the retchings of the deep.

The boundary of life and death
suspended in each breath:
illusion of the human mind.

Where nothing's as it seems.

IV

Jen watches television:
an in depth half an hour
on global warming's
strange new flowers
by our polluted streams.

Devastating droughts.
raging forest fires
that melt the ancient ice caps
thawing in their gleam.

Her friend says:
"But Britain will get warmer."

She replies:
"But that would mean no bluebells."

the woodlands start to steam.

That would mean no bluebells
or the insect life that tends it
as the ecosystem slips
for the sake of a sun tan sheen.

Land parched where once was green.

V

Richard and Judy,

brainless and broody,

are hosting children's fashion week.

"Too many boys

such little time."

Boasts Tina's top,

she's not quite nine.

And there's a bra and panty set

for five years olds - their daddy's pets.

Little beauty queens

not even in their teens.

VI

Dave used to be a happy chap

until he got a happy slap:

he'd passed his GCSE's

avoiding crack and smack and Es.

At least he's got a sort of fame:

he's on TV in Crime of the Week

in a hospital bed attached to a drain.

The doctor says the outlook's bleak.

Though he's asleep he doesn't dream.

VII

The forests burn

to make the pretty lights

that shine in Vegas.

But that would mean no bluebells.

Lord save us.

save us from this dream.

CHEMTRAIL

Little sky sperm
hurtling through the blue,
you do not bring life.

In your toxic wake
you leave a trail of sickness
as you scar the air
with your chemical knife.

POLLUTION

Dusty greyness
swaddles the airspace.
A microscope confirms
what the eye suspected:
chemical components
have modified the substance
formerly known as air.

As towns villages
become connected
in the filthy urban sprawl
the metallic tasting
all embracing
pollution gathers in.

"Trees filter
most of the poisons."
A mother's heard to say

whilst in the pram
her baby wears
a miniature dust mask:
"I don't know what this cough is
my lungs were healthy as a child.
I've never smoked and hold my breath
when traffic fumes pass by.
The doctor says its asthma
so I carry an inhaler.
It's worse I find in summer
but you never can be sure.

The Schizophrenic tramp
is seen as mad by urbanites.
But tramp schizo's always known
that's why he's gone insane
unable to deal with
deceit, corruption, industrial rain.

It's clear to him there's nothing wrong

except the filtering round his brain.
Perhaps they will devise
a mask for round his mind.

The young are the old tramp's friends:
they've travelled there
not unaware
through computer and designer drug
combined hallucinations.

They call this normal, all the same:
the habitat of the insane sane.

THE SNOWDROPS HAVE COME EARLY

The snowdrops have come early
my father mutters to the trees.

In the eaves a flash of mustard lime
and the blue tit's cap of beetle hue
twists in search of information
with lyric chatter, whistled song.

A yellow sun floats in seaside blue,
grey boats, the clouds, trail past
the masts of conifers.

Plant life's caught mid metamorphosis,
buds spiral out the branches
past death-mottled leaves
still clinging to a former incarnation.

The palette of this December's filled

with wintergreens and shades of sage and laurel.
The naked filigree of trees
look stifled in their cardigans of ivy.

The water runs clear and sharp
and squirrels find new ways to climb
to dispossess the robin of his feast
as the dunnock and the nuthatch scavenge
crumbs from yesterday.
Their monkish brown an echo of the sparrow
who's disappeared with old red squirrel,
preserved in stories and memory of childish years.
Though which is which I cannot always tell.

The clock strikes four and the lilac grey of twilight
is chimed into existence.
The old tick tock of the old oak clock
where past and future are fused in present;
the crackle of the wireless and the kettle's steam,
the ripple of a newspaper and half caught words

of war and preparations for war
already half dismissed.

My father turns to my mother:

"The snowdrops have come early."

WHEN THE BEES GO

Colony Collapse Disorder
recently observed:
the honeybees are dying,
their hive life is disturbed.

The honeybees pollinate
the flowers of the world
and when the honeybees are gone
no flowers will unfurl.

These little bees make honey
as they fertilise each flower;
if only they made money
they might retain their power.

GET INVOLVED

SOCIAL ACTION

It is time you started taking responsibility for your local area and start doing something out of the ordinary to establish a connection with society around you. Ditch the fear, get involved.

Stop whining about life and do something positive yourself. Start setting an example in your community that says you don't have to accept the status quo or wait for someone else to challenge it – if you want to see a change in your area make it happen now. Throw caution to the wind and dance the fig leaf fandango at Tesco's. Ask the vicar. Turn it into a tradition.

Far too many communities have been robbed of their independence and communal strength through the culture of dependency that grew up under God's Big Government and Social Action is one of the ways you can start to work for and with your local communities to change that.

So ditch the deity and fill the vacancy. My track record speaks for itself. It was me that gave you your self-awareness. It was me that first understood you and encouraged you to stop all that pointless guilt. And it is me offering you Knowledge and Life as promises in my manifesto. And unlike the opposition I am not going to threaten you with consequences.

I'm not going to bang on about morals. I'm not trying to impress or be anyone other than myself. Just don't believe everything you've heard about me. Those rumours about me being some sort of horny beast are ghastly slurs spread by the opposition. That's bad press from the last by-election. I never said I was a saint.

BIG BULLY

Evil seems to triumph.

It does not.

Just makes a big noise,
a violent bully in this realm.
The ultimate coward
and small town thug.

All the other universes
stay calm, composed
where it lingers as a ghost.

WAY THROUGH THE WOODS

There's a way through the woods
in the cool light of winter
that twists like a root that curves by the stream.
though dark there's a green light
that glows through the lichen
which grows on the stones by the banks of the stream
and brittle brown leaves burnt on the bushes
have burned out their light which was gold in the fall.
And the trees are all sleeping like bears in the cold
    nights
and all you can hear is the trickling water's
crisp liquid voice from treble to bass
as it falls down the hill to the path by the stream.
The trees throw arabesque filigree branches
on a dull opal sky not luminous quite
but I'm free on the path that winds through the forest
I can still find my way in the plain winter light.

THE DANDY IN THE SKY

A drop of liquid light
targets the horizon
with solar chromatography.

Veils of rose organza
trail in fluid turquoise,
glowing through lilac:
a fantasy prism,
wordless in wonder
at the special effects
of planetary motion.

The trill on a Copernican tune.

The first stars glisten
their diamond solitaires
as flamingo-purple hazes
trail across a lemon moon

still filling up, rising
against the sapphires of the sky.

Jewels of the kaleidoscope
slip and shift to heliotrope;
fractals of the sun
eloping with night,
delighting the dusk
with ruby and cerulean.
Russets, indigo and golden tones
flicker the sky dome
with mother-of-pearl.

The symphony concludes:

Transparencies of aquamarine,
overlaid with tangerine
and rainbow sheens of tourmaline,
slide into violet and twilight.